No 1

The Flamedam Fire
Meditations for children
Gitte Winter Graugaard

The Clear Cascade
Meditations for children

The Deep Meadow
Meditations for children

Meet Chief Eaglefeather
Meditations for children
Gitte Winter Graugaard

The Mild Winds
Meditations for children
Gitte Winter Graugaard

THIS IS BOOK ONE IN THE SERIES **THE VALLEY OF HEARTS**
An amazing series of books with child meditations
written by Gitte Winter Graugaard. Show your child how to reach
their inner valley. "Meet Chief Eaglefeather" (no 1) and let him
teach you to use the four elements: Fire, Water, Earth, and Air.
Help your child cleanse their own energy with "The Flamedancers'
Fire" (no 2). Cleanse off other people's energies under "The Clear
Cascade" (no 3). Find peace in "The Deep Meadow" (no 4).
Fly high to get new perspective on "The Mild Winds" (no 5).

www.thevalleyofhearts.com

#kidsmeditate

To

____

____

Your personal note to the
child you give this book to

____

____

____

____

From

____

____

Meet Chief Eaglefeather
Meditations for children

By Gitte Winter Graugaard

Illustrations by
Elsie Ralston

Room for Reflection Publishing

The purpose of this book is not to give medical advice, nor to give a prescription for the use of any technique as a form of treatment for any physical, medical, psychological, or emotional condition.

The information in this book does not replace the advice of a physician, either directly or indirectly. It is intended only as general information and education. In the event that you use any of the information in this book for yourself, as is your constitutional right, the author and publisher assume no responsibility for your actions. No expressed or implied guarantee of the effect of use of any of the recommendations can be given. The author and publisher are not liable or responsible for any loss or damage allegedly arising from any information in this book.

Without limiting the rights under copyright reserved above, no part of this publication may be reproduced, stored in, or introduced into a retrieval system, or transmitted in any form or by any means (electronic, mechanical, photocopying, recording, or otherwise), without the prior written permission of the copyright owner.

The scanning, uploading, and distribution of this book via the Internet or any other means without the permission of the publisher is illegal and punishable by law.

Please purchase only authorized electronic or printed editions, and do not participate in or encourage any electronic piracy of copyrightable materials. Your support of the author's rights is appreciated. When you support a passionate soul you ignite her fire and help her change the world into a better place.

While the author has made every effort to provide accurate information regarding references and Internet addresses at the time of publication, the author does not assume responsibility for errors or changes that occur after publication. The author also does not assume any responsibility for third-party websites and/or their content.

Meet Chief Eaglefeather © 2021 Gitte Winter Graugaard

"Teaching our children to reconnect to nature is a gift for life. Let's teach them how fire, water, earth and air create balance and work together. By mirroring their behaviour we can find inner peace."

- Gitte Winter Graugaard

The books in the series The Valley of Hearts are:
- Meet Chief Eaglefeather
- The Flamedancers' Fire
- The Clear Cascade
- The Deep Meadow
- The Mild Winds

Other books published in English:
- The Children's Meditations In my Heart
- Heartlight – teach your child to shine

The series will be available in several
languages in the future.

See where we're at with our words here:
www.gittewintergraugaard.dk

♡ ♡ ♡

My dear reader

Thank you for finding your way to The Valley of Hearts. And thank you for bringing children to the valley with you. I wish you a magical time with all of us heart people in the valley. We can't wait to see you and make you feel at home. Home is where the heart is, and this valley is so full of love.

Much love
Gitte Winter Graugaard

www.thevalleyofhearts.com

♡ ♡ ♡

Meet Chief Eaglefeather, Meditations for Children
A book from the series The Valley of Hearts
Copyright © Gitte Winter Graugaard 2021
1st edition in English 2021

Author: Gitte Winter Graugaard
Illustrations: Elsie Ralston
Layout: Katrine Høyer
Translation: Eva Juul, Gitte Winter Graugaard
Editor: Sam Jennings

ISBN: 978-87-93210-54-7 (paperback)
ISBN: 978-87-93210-55-4 (hardbound)
ISBN: 978-87-93210-56-1 (e-book)
ISBN: 978-87-93210-57-8 (PDF)

Room for Reflection Publishing

Table of contents

Introduction 11

How to read the book 19

Let me introduce the two meditations

Introduction to Arriving in The Valley 27

Introduction to Meet Chief Eaglefeather 29

Let's meditate

Meditation 1 33

Meditation 2 45

Your notes 52

Reflections after meeting Eaglefeather 57

About the author 62

About the illustrator 63

Be creative - colouring... 67

Your notes 90

About the book series The Valley of Hearts 96

A Global Mission...101

Let me introduce you
to the valley and the wise
Chief Eaglefeather

Introduction

I believe that all children are born as light and love and have
come to this wonderful planet to thrive. However, little by little our
experiences at home or at school, teach us to dim our light in some
way or another and we veer off of our natural path. Meditation can
bring us back on track and remind us, we are all full of love and light
and that we have a strong connection with Mother Nature.

Sadly, many children suffer from nature deficit. Not being in nature
enough is a much bigger problem for us than we might think. There
is so much innate wisdom hidden in nature to which we have lost
access. And the sense that we ourselves also ARE nature is no longer
natural. This I believe is the reason why we have seen a rise in mental
health problems all over the world, both in children and adults.

Obviously, urbanisation and industrialisation are partly to blame
for why we have forgotten the fundamental role nature plays in our
wellbeing. Having easy access to so many activities and services in
the cities so that we no longer depend on nature, is of course very
convenient, but it also means we miss out on a lot of healing and
peace afforded to us by nature, both outside of us and from within.

Our strong desire to dominate and be efficient as human beings has
in many ways separated us from our source of life - Mother Nature.
We all have a multitude of natural resources hidden inside of us.
However, we have a tendency to lose sight of them, especially when
stressed. This is also true for our children.

At school, we learn little of our mind, body and heart connections.
And how do we as parents teach our children about their inner
worlds if we've lost touch with our own?

Bring your child to The Valley of Hearts and show them a natural way
of finding peace, balance and harmony. With this series of books, you
can teach your child how to find their inner strength and understand

and regulate their emotions. Teach your child about their inner landscape and where to go to find strength, balance, resource, love, and light.

The meditations in The Valley of Hearts unfold against the backdrop of a fictive indigenous valley. Your child is met by the wise *Chief Eaglefeather*, and is invited to explore with him the four natural elements around and within us:

- Fire

- Water

- Earth

- Air

Chief Eaglefeather taps into our innate wisdom of nature, stored in our collective consciousness, and makes us reconnect with nature again.

He is from everywhere and nowhere exactly. He has been carried through generations through storytelling and intuition. He knows all oceans, all mountains, all continents, and all native cultures. He is a friend to all children. He is not a religious character – albeit love is his religion should we choose one for him.

Listen

Our language comprises many expressions that illustrate our intuitive and natural knowledge about the elements. We understand when a passionate person "is on fire". We see the effect of a message "resonating like ripples in water". We might feel we need "grounding" or are in need of "a change of air". Once you begin to examine the elements in greater detail, you will soon find many sayings and words embedded within our diverse languages that make reference to them.

I was inspired to write the series of meditations in The Valley of Hearts after meeting many of the children who had read my earlier book The Children's Meditations in my Heart. As more and more children told me about their Love Mountains and showed me their drawings of their beautiful hearts deep within their mountains, it occurred to me that together we had co-created a whole range of love mountains, spanning north to south and from east to west. I closed my eyes and imagined what life would be like in the valley beneath that beautiful, loving mountain range and this series of books came to me.

A gift for life

We often don't need to "teach" meditation to children. They are already much more mindful than us. But the older they get, the more they are affected by society's busy energy and the more they need to be reminded of how beautiful they are inside and that they are much stronger than they often realise.

Meditation can help them get to know their inner world, strength, beauty and power. To know about meditation from an early age is a gift for life.

In today's hectic society, where children receive a large amount of information through multiple channels simultaneously, the unique still and quiet of contemplation is precious. By using the meditations in this series of books, you train your child to immerse, contemplate and use their imagination to become more creative and innovative.

I also warmly welcome professionals to use these meditations in school or with groups of children. This series of books can be read aloud to children from the age of five and well into their teens.

With these books, we help children find inner peace and balance, and at the same time, create lovely, mindful moments of togetherness in families and at school. Thank you for being curious about methods that may seem alternative but have been here for thousands of years. The book is also wonderful for children to use in yoga classes structured around the elements with physical exercises that help children connect to the elements.

Therapy in nature

All my life I have been drawn towards nature. As a child I loved being outdoors. The garden of my childhood home was enchanting, with lots of nooks, crannies and hiding places, not to mention beautiful flowers, ripe fruit and juicy berries, wild bushes and ancient trees.

My mother was always to be found weeding somewhere in our huge, never-ending garden. In the summertime we literally lived in the garden, and used to hoist our meals in a large basket on a rope from the kitchen window onto the garden.

My father had built a large barbeque and we had a fireplace in the back garden. We jumped joyfully from our swings into, what seemed to be, the largest sandpit in the world.

Together my sister, my friends and I built secret caves in the back of the garden. We slept in tents, made bonfires, grilled twisted bread on sticks, tossed balls over the roof of our skyhigh house, earned a penny mowing the lawn, and in the wintertime, we built snowmen with carrots for noses and my father's old scarves around their necks. I was a girl scout and I learned that nature is one big playground! The elements fire, water, earth and air played a big role in my upbringing.

Connection

I strongly believe that a closer connection to, and a better understanding of the elements in nature inside of us can also help save our planet. The sooner we begin to understand that we belong in nature, that we are nature, the more likely we are to take better care of it. And we know kids are the best caretakers of nature. They need only a little reminding and often they question the way we do things from what we in mindfulness call "the beginner's mind", which occurs when we see or understand things for the first time. Why do we kill animals? Why do people throw plastic into the ocean? Why are they cutting trees in my forest? All of these are natural questions for children to ask. Listen to your child. They know. Let them make you want to make a difference too.

Why did we forget in the first place?

While scientists investigate the effect of natural therapy, as for instance seen in Stress Therapy Gardens in Sweden and Forest Bathing in Japan, most of us already know that nature is good for our souls and minds.

In Denmark we have quite a few forest kindergartens, where children spend all hours outside. And we see more families moving to the countryside as a conscious choice to create better balance by letting their children grow up in touch with nature.

Could we change those scary statistics on stress in children and adolescents by teaching them meditation and reconnection with nature? And would they then look after our planet in a better way? I strongly believe so, yes.

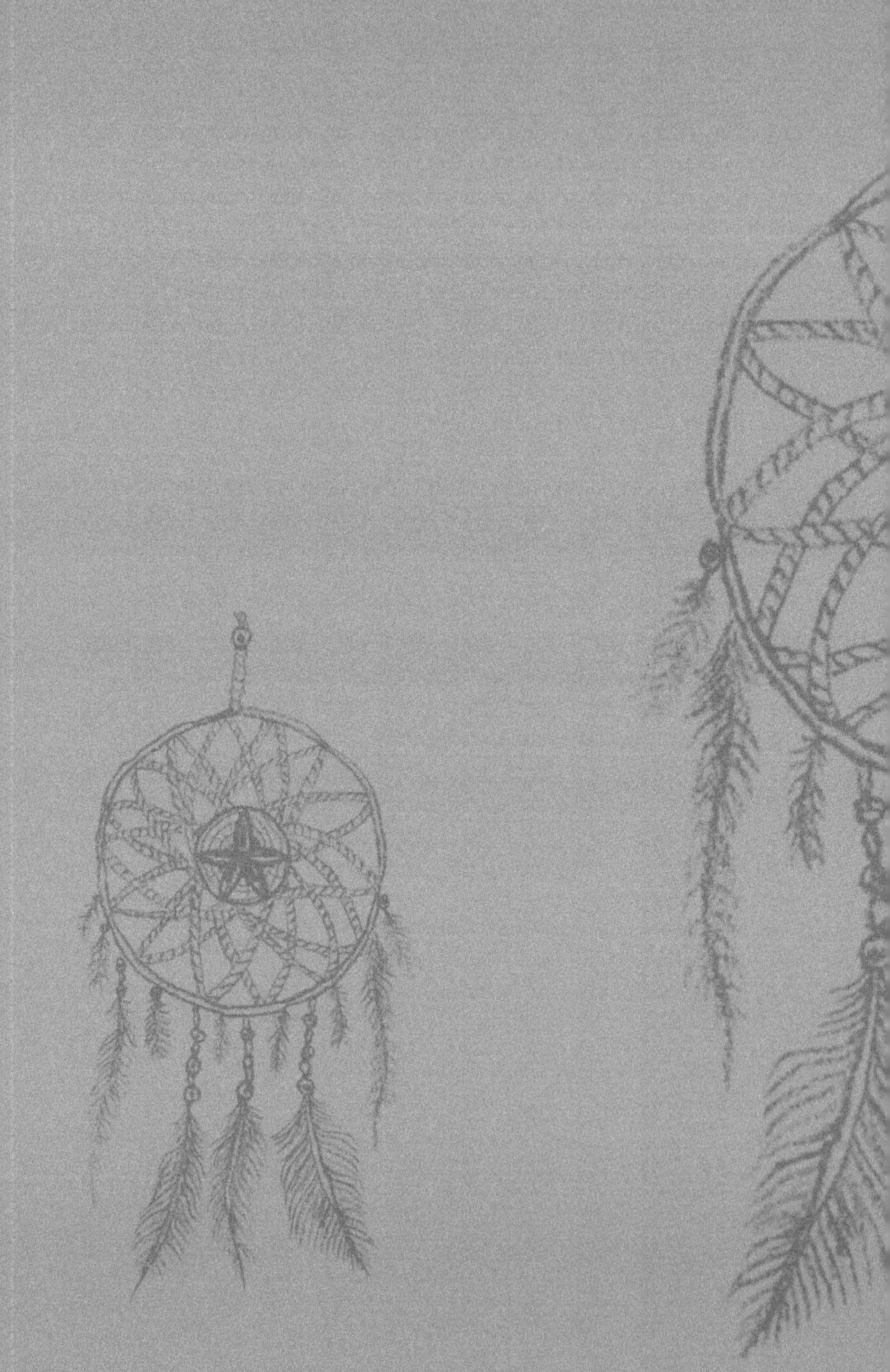

How to read the books

The meditations in each book are guided visualisations, which you and your child co-create together with *Chief Eaglefeather*. As you guide your child into the meditations with closed eyes, your child will delve deeper into the sceneries and energies of the book. And by the use of their breathing, senses and imagination, your child can find all the magic inside themselves, whilst you read aloud.

If you are new to child meditation this is a different way of both storytelling and listening. If you are already acquainted with my book *'The Children's Meditations in my Heart'*, the books will be an easy follow-up for you, as your child will already be familiar with the format.

If this is a new concept for you both, your child might need to get used to it. Take your time and be patient. Your calmness and presence when reading aloud are essential for your child's experience.

Whilst reading, you will see three hearts:

They signal when I recommend you pause and give your child time to contemplate.

You will also be encouraged to make your child the main character of the meditation, by mentioning the child's name whenever you find an open, underlined space in the text _______________.
Feel free to mention your child by name more often, if you sense that it inspires them.

When you encounter areas of text in italics or (brackets) midpage in the meditation, it is a small message offering you alternatives.

It is a good idea for you to read through the meditations before reading them to your child. This enables you to be completely present with them when reading aloud. And if you feel like making changes to the text, feel free to do so. You intuitively know what will serve your child best.

Use your senses

We all process information differently and we may use different senses to do so. Hence, the meditations are filled with sensory stimulation, each appealing to different impressions.

Some children will activate a feeling by way of the smell from a bonfire, others by listening to a cascading waterfall, some will envisage the camp. Some might also recognise the feel of various materials on their skin.

Be curious about the senses your child accesses during meditation. When you discover your child's preferred sense, add more of the words that tap into your child's favourite sensory stimulation. This will help your child expand their imagination and explore their inner world more intently. No one sense is better than another.

The art lies in teaching ourselves and our children, to acknowledge and become aware of what works and what creates balance for each and every one of us.

Keep calm

Please pay attention to your own energy before and whilst reading aloud. Maybe your energy is low. Or your child isn't in the mood to be read to, can't lay still, doesn't want this book or refuses to close their eyes. All these disturbances might impact you in a negative way. However, try to keep calm and pass on a loving energy and intention.

It is quite alright if your child will not close their eyes immediately. It can be hard to let go after a day full of stimulation. If you work with several children or a larger group, it might take a while for them to calm down and close their eyes.

Some children feel vulnerable when closing their eyes and can be a bit scared to do so. This is a natural instinct from ancient times. So be patient and keep calm.

You can ask those children to instead focus on a certain spot somewhere in the room, whilst repeating from time to time and without pressure, that whenever he or she is content and willing, it would be good to close their eyes.

You might have to read the meditations several times before the last child closes his eyes. This is fine and perfectly okay. Once you get there, it will be a small victory for the child to have found this form of comfort in your group. If this is the case, do remember to give the child credit.

It is also normal for a child to move around during the meditation. When we let go of our conscious mind and transfer our focus to our body, it can feel nice to shift the energies around.

If you feel yourself getting irritated or impatient, take a couple of deep breaths to re-find your own inner peace. Just repeat calmly and peacefully: "Lie down comfortably, close your eyes and enjoy this special moment." In a larger group, it can also be expected that some children will fidget for a while.

If one or more children are particularly uneasy, it might help if you gently touch their bodies, beginning with their arms to see if the child likes it.

You could also commence the session by letting the children massage each other. The unease might arise, because the children have difficulty sensing their own bodies or are not used to meditating.

Child massage or caressing might enhance their body awareness. All children are different and there is no right or wrong way to meditate. One of my daughters often turns herself around 10 times before settling down, while the other lies quietly like a mouse.

When reading the meditation aloud, the most important thing is that you stay calm and that the meditation comes from a loving place from within.

Guidance for you

- Make sure that you yourself are calm and radiating love before reading. It will be a challenge to create an atmosphere of peace and calm if you are not in balance.

- Remember to breathe deeply, all the way down to your belly, whilst reading. Take an extra deep breath if you get annoyed with your child, or lose focus.

- Read slowly and pause during the reading. Leave your child time to use their imagination.

- Accept intruding noise, if any. We can't stop the turmoil of the world, but we can learn to navigate it.

It is perfectly alright if your child falls asleep. If you feel like it take a nap yourself. While snoozing you will be nourished and re-energised.

If your child finds falling asleep difficult, this might just be the book you need.

Dream creation

Enjoy this special moment with your child. It is amazing that you are able to introduce these magnificent tools to your child.

Imagine that you are both seated in front of a giant dream loom. The colours and energies of these meditations are the colourful threads you can use to weave the first part of your child's dreams as you embark on your adventure into The Valley of Hearts.

Together you weave the first rows that shape the beginning of your child's dreams, and will influence how the dream "meanders" during the night.

Dreams affect the quality of your child's sleep and have great impact on how your child wakes up the next day.

From research we know that the brain waves during meditation resemble the activity in the brain during REM sleep. By meditating before bedtime, we begin the mind cleansing work that sleep helps us to do.

Let me introduce
the two meditations

Introduction to 'Arriving in The Valley'

'Arriving in The Valley' is one of two preliminary meditations written to introduce your child to The Valley of Hearts, before you move on to the four elements in the next books (if you choose to do so). Once your child feels comfortable in the valley, curiosity to venture further in and to explore the elements will come more readily.

I recommend you always allow your child enough time to arrive in The Valley of Hearts. In doing so, you will activate the calm, deep breathing that enables your child to shift their focus from conscious thinking in the brain to the physical fatigue of the body.

I also recommend you read the book as a bedtime story. Generally, we are kept awake at bedtime by thinking and sometimes over-thinking, although the body is actually exhausted. By transferring your focus to inside your body, you enhance the feeling of fatigue and make it easier to fall asleep.

Please be aware that every day can be different in terms of how long it takes for your child to find peace, feel their body and consequently, enter The Valley of Hearts.

Once you are familiar with this first meditation, you may shorten it and move on to talking about Chief Eaglefeather and then one of the four the elements in the other books.

However, don't forget that most children enjoy repetition and therefore, might love hearing the longer introduction.

At the end of this first meditation there are various endings to choose from, all dependent on what feels right at the time of reading.

Keep in mind you need to activate your own deep and soothing breathing.

Introduction to:
Meet Chief Eaglefeather

Once you have arrived in The Valley of Hearts using the previous meditation, you are ready to meet your guide: the kind, wise and patient, Chief Eaglefeather. He can become a very important character in your child's life, a friend who teaches them how to find balance in their every day.

He lives in the valley, and the elements fire, water, earth and air are his allies.

Chief Eaglefeather encounters all children with the same enthusiasm, and makes them all feel unique and welcome in the valley. It enhances the child's self-assurance if you make Chief Eaglefeather's greeting of your child something special, every time your child arrives in the valley.

If you are familiar with characteristics you know your child would appreciate to find in Chief Eaglefeather, feel free to add them to his character. The more generous, loving and kind you can make him, the more comfort your child will derive from being in his company.

Chief Eaglefeather gives you a tour of the camp, and introduces you to the four elements. Please note that Chief Eaglefeather always participates in the practices, and in doing so, this makes him feel better every time. Let it be an invitation to you too, to cleanse your own spirit as well. If not concurrently with your child, then afterwards, or better still, before you start meditating with your child.

You will find more encouragements for reflection for you as parent or caregiver after the meditation.

Let's meditate

Arriving in The Valley

Arriving in The Valley of Hearts

Dear_______________________ (insert NAME or "children" if you have more listeners).

Deep down in the tummies of all children we can find a very special place called The Valley of Hearts. You get there by taking deep breaths. Come, let's try together. Let's try to reach the valley and go on an inner adventure.

You have so much magic inside of you and I would love to introduce you to this magic. Because, once you know just how beautiful and strong you are inside, life becomes both easier and more magical. And all I really wish for you is to see your life as magical.

When you are ready, lie or sit down comfortably. Settle down and cover up with a blanket if you like. Make yourself comfortable. Feel the ground under you. Connect to the ground.

Focus your attention on your breathing.

Breathe in through your nose, and out through your mouth. Calmly. Find your inner peace. This special moment is all yours. Right here and right now, you don't have to perform, to pretend, or to look in a particular way. In The Valley of Hearts you are welcome - just the way you are. You are loved for being you.

Try to follow the air that you breathe in through the nose, down the throat, to your lungs and your tummy, and all the way back up until you blow it out through your mouth or nose again.

Close your eyes when you are ready.

(If your child won't close their eyes, try saying the following: "If you are not ready to close your eyes yet, please find a spot in the ceiling or on the wall upon which to focus. Once you feel ready, then close your eyes.")

The adventure in The Valley of Hearts becomes even more magical when you close your eyes. This enables you to create your own visions by using your imagination.

You might hear sounds from this room or from outside. Listen to them.

Also try to catch any sounds from yourself, or maybe even from inside yourself.

Maybe your tummy rumbles a little? Or maybe you can hear your own breathing?

Your body is active 24/7, but when, as now, it is allowed to lie still, it might produce little cosy sounds, as if telling you that it appreciates the peace and quiet. Take a moment to listen to the sounds, and then let them all slip away and listen to my voice instead.

If you feel like yawning, take a deep long yawn. Yawning is the body telling us that it's time to wind down and seek peace.
Your body needs to rest during the day as well as during the night.

Finding inner peace by breathing deeply is your access to The Valley of Hearts. Within a short while, when you are completely calm, maybe with your eyes closed, and your body completely relaxed, you will find your way. I hope you are excited about your journey into the valley. I am.

Okay, let's begin our arrival to The Valley of Hearts. Wiggle your toes or squeeze my hand when you are ready to come along.

(Allow your child to signal that he or she is ready).

Now that your breathing is quite deep, and you are delightfully calm, our trip to the magnificent and lush Valley of Hearts can begin.

In this story you are the main character. This story is all about you and your beauty inside.

I will ever so slowly start telling you about life in a small tepee camp in The Valley of Hearts, the most enchanting place you can possibly imagine. Maybe by now you have already noticed that in a meditation you get to decide the colours and details.

You have now arrived in the valley. Imagine that you are standing in an exquisite meadow surrounded by the most magnificent mountains.

Imagine it to be the most beautiful summer's day. A blue sky above you with the summer sun hanging high in the sky, warming your lovely body. A slight breeze bids you welcome. Try to feel the breeze on your skin.

Try to visualise the meadow you are standing in with your inner eye. It is green and lush and smells like fresh earth after a summer rainfall.

Listen! Right in front of you a river is flowing by. Can you hear the rippling? Can you smell the fresh water? The river bids you welcome to The Valley of Hearts. The whole valley is so happy that YOU decided to come for a visit ____________________.

The wise old river twists its way through deep meadows under the high mountains of The Valley of Hearts. Now I am going to tell you something very special about the water in this amazing river. It originates from the very top of the mountains surrounding the valley. The mountains are called The Love Mountains.

The mountains stand so tall, that in the wintertime their peaks are covered by a soft, white blanket of snow. You know the kind of snow that melts on your tongue and has the softest velvety feeling on your cheek; the kind of gentle snow that allows you to play the most enthralling winter games.

When summer comes and the warm rays of the big old sun dance on the peaks anew, the snow slowly melts, and finds its way down the mountains. Some of these creeks assemble in marvellous little rippling brooks, whilst others become surging waterfalls, all meeting up in the river in the valley. One of the waterfalls you will come to know as The Clear Cascade.

In The Valley of Hearts something else, something very special, also makes the snow melt. This happens even on the coldest of winter days when icicles adorn the trees and a clear moon dances in the frost-clear, star-laden night sky.

Now listen carefully. Because every single one of these beautiful Love Mountains in The Valley of Hearts belongs to a child, just like you, somewhere in the world. And inside each mountain lives the love from the heart of that child.

This is why we call the mountains in The Valley of Hearts the Love Mountains.

And will you believe this? The heat generated from children filling their hearts with love makes the snow melt and cascade down the mountains to merge with the waterfalls and the rivers below. Isn't that amazing?

You too have a Love Mountain. Maybe you're already familiar with it? If not I might tell you about it another day.

So when you hear the river roaring through the valley, and you clearly see that the water is crystal clear and clean, you will realise that the water of the river, right here in the valley, holds a special magic. Special because it is sourced from the snow on top of the Love Mountains and infused with a love so pure. Because nothing in the whole wide world is as pure as the love of a child!

So here you are now, standing barefoot in the grass, on the riverbank, surrounded by the Love Mountains, on this warm summer's day. Look around you and sense the atmosphere. When collecting love from all the children of the world in a valley like The Valley of Hearts, surely it must be a most extraordinary place to be. Can you feel the love they share with you?

On the opposite side of the roaring river, you might see a row of tepee tents in a camp. You might also notice a column of smoke rising from a bonfire.

The camp is inhabited by very special people living in beautiful tepees. Breathe in the peaceful atmosphere of the camp and sense the happiness of the people living there. Tepees are a sort of tent built from slim rafters, assembled at the top and spread out in a circle at the ground. Over the rafters the people have wrapped a piece of coarse canvas, sewn on with a cord to find shelter.

Try to imagine the tepee. Maybe yours has wonderful colours and patterns?

In front of you, you see a small bridge, made of rocks, that leads across the river. With a lightness in your body you jump from rock to rock.

As you cross the river you discover more of the valley's magic. The river seems to talk to you and bids you welcome. Listen carefully to what it says: "Welcome child, it's wonderful to see you! ", the river roars.

You might already sense that your imagination is a marvellous travel partner, when venturing into The Valley of Hearts.

You sense that the rocks are worn flat on the top, and are quite easy to walk on. This is due to the many children that have crossed the river before you. Every night many children arrive in the valley, and they too cross the river using this bridge.

This means that you children show each other the way into the valley!

As you approach the camp, you see children playing. Some are similar to you. Others have a different skin colour, hair style, or are wearing a different type of clothing. Some are tall, others short, some are chubby, others thin. If you see a child in a wheelchair, please ask if you can help push them along in the valley.

There are young children as well as teenagers, boys and girls all playing together. You sense a kinship and happiness amongst them, and feel like moving closer to them. In The Valley of Hearts all children are equal, and all children are welcome.

Try to smell the smoke from the bonfires in the camp now that we are closer to it.

Try to catch the sound of the river roaring past in the background. Maybe you can also hear the children's voices from the camp.

Can you still feel the rays of the sun on your skin?

No matter where you turn in the valley, you sense a warm and loving ambience. This place is filled with the most ravishing magic, making us humans particularly joyous. And how could it be otherwise, now that we are so close to The Love Mo untains?

All the children of the world have access to The Valley of Hearts, but only a few know about it yet. So consider yourself lucky to have already found the way to this magnificent spot!

Dearest__________________________. Welcome to *The Valley of Hearts*. May you have many magical moments in this beautiful valley. May it become very dear to you. May you grow up knowing you have this valley inside of you and may it become your symbol that you too are fire, water, earth and air.

Choose an ending:

Is the child going to sleep?

You are now ready to drift off into a wonderful sleep after your visit to *The Valley of Hearts*. Sleep tight with sweet dreams about the many magical fairy tales of the valley.

Are you moving on to the next meditation in this book?
Now that you are familiar with the valley, we are ready to move on. If you are ready for more experiences in the valley, wiggle your toes or squeeze my hand.

Is the child continuing their day?
The time has come to start moving your toes and fingers and to slowly return to this room. After this quiet moment we are now ready to encounter the rest of the day. In our hearts, we can bring with us all of our lovely experiences in *The Valley of Hearts*.

Meet Chief
Eaglefeather

Meet Chief Eaglefeather

(Before reading this story, I recommend that you let your child arrive in the valley by way of the first meditation).

As you explore the camp, you soon notice a very special man on a small rock by the riverside. He stands tall and proud, with one foot in front of the other on the cliff. His muscles are distinct and his cheekbones pronounced.

He sees you too, and breaks into a wide smile. Swiftly he jumps down from the rock, and walks cheerfully towards you. His clothing is bright and covered in the most magnificent patterns of all colours, the ones you love the most.

On his head he carries an impressive collection of the most amazing eagle feathers you can imagine.

He is a strong and handsome man. His raven black hair hangs long, loose and straight down his back, flowing gently in the wind as he walks towards you.

Standing right in front of you with a big smile and friendly eyes, he says:

"Hello sweet________________________________ Welcome to The Valley of Hearts, I have really been looking forward to seeing you. I am fortunate to live in a very magical camp with a lot of lovely friends and family.

Every day we are visited by children - just like you - from all over the world. When I saw that it was you arriving today, I was so happy," he continues.

"I am Chief Eaglefeather," he says and extends his hand to greet you. "You are always welcome to visit me and all my friends here in The Valley of Hearts. You are my friend and I can be yours if you want me to be," he says, smiling warmly at you.

You immediately feel comfortable with Chief Eaglefeather and you are curious to know him. You notice his eyes. There is something about them, something extraordinary. They sparkle bright like ten thousand stars in the sky. It feels like you can glide into them, and in there, deep down, magnificently, you somehow recognise yourself.

"Come along, let me show you around our marvellous camp," Chief Eaglefeather says with a smile, and gives you the chance to hold his hand.

"There are many magical elements in this camp. I want to show you four of them that I know you will cherish. You are already familiar with them. We all are. But somehow many people today have forgotten they also have the elements inside of them.

The four elements I will show you are my friends and helpers: Fire, Water, Earth and Air. These elements are magical components of our nature. I want to show you the elements, and hope you will cherish them just as much as I do.

Now, I will tell you where to find the four elements in the valley so that later on, you can choose which to visit to feel their magic. Each one has a unique character that can help us find balance and live a meaningful life."

"Right over here in our camp we have a very exceptional bonfire, with the most exquisite blaze. The powerful logs carry the dancing blue, red and yellow-orange flames. The flames are the magical elements of the fire that has been passed on for generations and the fire never goes out – just like our inner fire is always lit, even when everything looks rather dark in our lives.

But there is more. The fire is known to us as The Flamedancers' Fire. If you choose to visit the fire with me later on, I will tell you why we call it so, and teach you about the magic of The Flamedancers. They teach us about our inner fire. Maybe you already feel the energy of the fire inside of you. Try to connect to your inner fire. What does your inner fire look like?"

"When we walk through the meadow behind the camp, heading for the mountains, we will soon hear the roar of a waterfall, and here we will meet the element water.

When we approach closer still, you will notice that the waterfall is crystal clear. This, you may remember, is because the water comes from the snow on the top of The Love Mountains.

I look forward to teaching you about The Clear Cascade, if you come to visit me again. And you will understand the wonderful magic of the source, as it roars down through the waterfall and teaches us to cleanse our energy and fill ourselves with love. Maybe you can already feel the waterfall cleansing you now? Let the water run through your body to cleanse you."

"Behind the camp lies The Deep Meadow. With its peaceful slow breath, it invites us to learn about the magical element earth. As a human we are born to connect to the earth and feel grounded.

The hustle and bustle of everyday life can make us feel disconnected. But please know that you can always reconnect with Mother Earth in The Deep Meadow. I have played in the meadow since I was a little child, and still now, as an adult, I visit the meadow daily to find peace."

Maybe you already now feel the deep peace from the meadow? Maybe you feel a bit more relaxed by thinking about the meadow? Maybe you feel more sleepy?

"Later, we will advance further into the meadow, and soon you will encounter a small hill. By way of beautiful winding paths we will climb to the top, where we'll meet my family of eagles.

They will take us up to The Mild Winds, the magical element air. Come along on the most beautiful adventure.

Flying high above the camp, carried on along by The Mild Winds, you might get new perspectives, new ideas and become more creative."

Maybe you already feel a sense of a change of air in you? Maybe you feel lighter already?

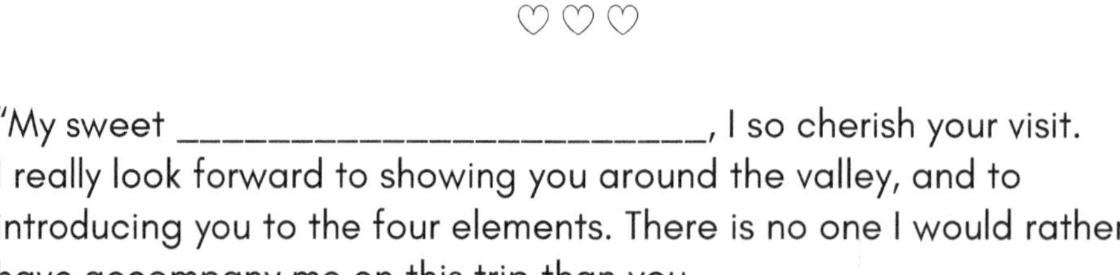

"My sweet ______________________________, I so cherish your visit.
I really look forward to showing you around the valley, and to introducing you to the four elements. There is no one I would rather have accompany me on this trip than you.

You might already know which of the four elements in the valley you feel like visiting. It can be really nice to visit all elements one after the other, but you will soon notice that you might be more drawn towards one or two of the elements over the rest. And this is what happens to most people. However, bear in mind there is so much for us to learn from all four elements," says Chief Eaglefeather.

Choose an ending

If you want to let your child stay a little longer:

Now, let us move on to the magical elements, and give you a chance to play with all the other children in the valley. Come, let's find your favoured element of the day.

If the child is going to sleep:

Dear_______________________________, now that you have met Chief Eaglefeather, it is time to go to sleep. Remember that you are always welcome to return and visit The Valley of Hearts. I so enjoyed visiting the valley with you today. I can't wait for us to do so again soon. Sweet dreams, sleep tight.

If the child is going on with their day:

Dear_______________________________, now that you have met Chief Eaglefeather, the time has come to return to this room. Start by moving your fingers and wiggle your toes up and down. When you are ready, open your eyes.

Remember that you can always come back and visit Chief Eaglefeather whenever you want to.

Notes on your experiences.

Did you all sleep better after meditating?

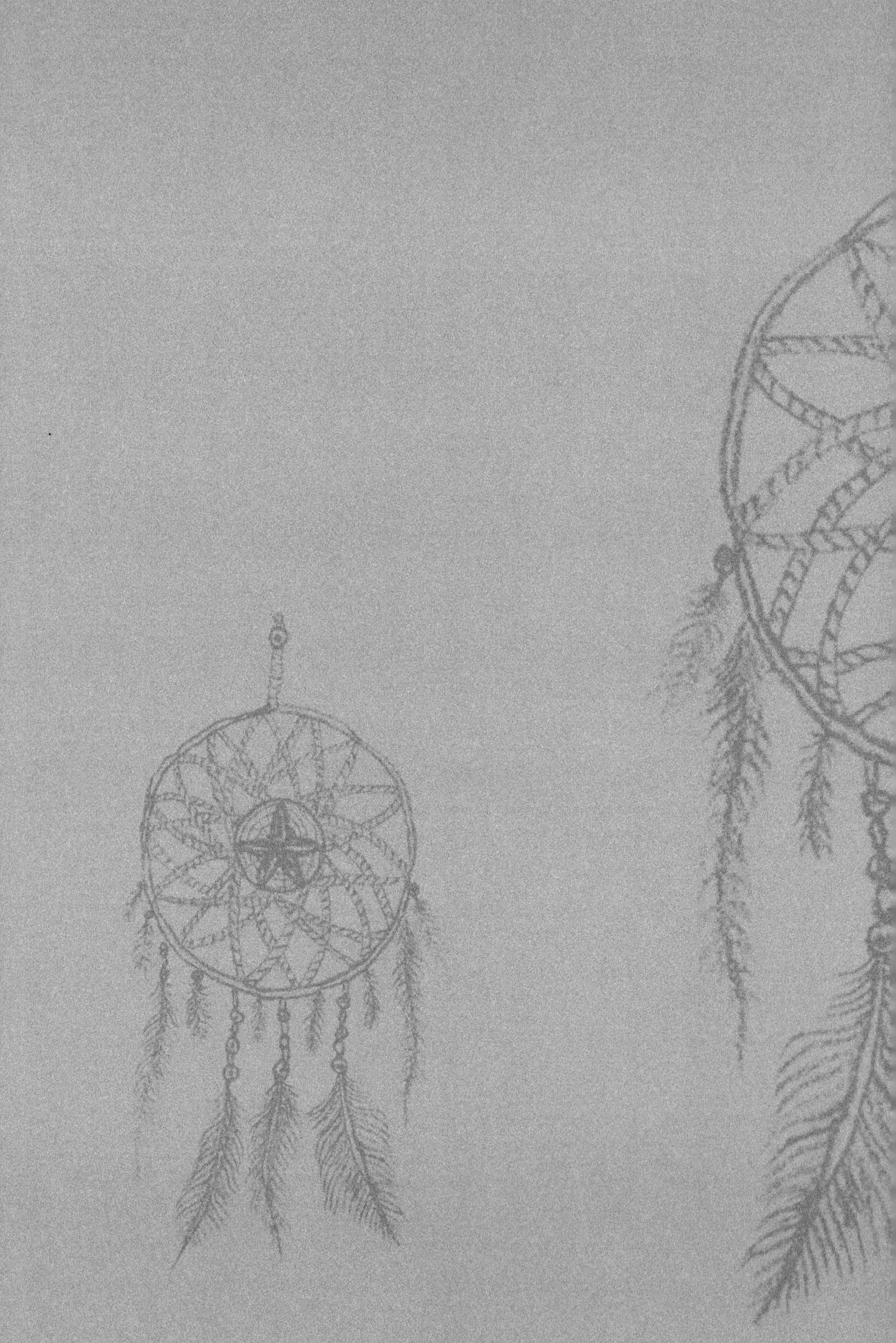

Let's go deeper

Reflections after meeting Chief Eaglefeather

- for you, the reader

I hope both you and your child have enjoyed meeting Chief Eaglefeather and will allow him to become a good friend.

Throughout the meditations in the books in this series, you will get to know him even better. But allow me to attach a few comments to him and encourage you to further reflection.

Listen to your child

Chief Eaglefeather symbolises an awareness that lies deep within us all. His guiding words, and working with the elements together, often feels completely natural to us, and especially to children. Chief Eaglefeather gives us access to an inner wisdom. You might discover your child finds it much easier to connect with this natural wisdom than you do. This is because children are still so open in their energies and consequently, don't have to fight their way around "brain land" as much as we adults do. They also tend to have better access to their imagination.

I heartily recommend you talk to your child about their experience with Chief Eaglefeather in The Valley of Hearts. You might feel like drawing the valley or/and Chief Eaglefeather. You will also find black and white drawings to colour in at the end of this book.

In the days following a meditation, as you talk about your experiences in the valley, try to be extra alert and observe which details your child registers and pays attention to. Be mindful of the senses that seem to play a role in your child's comprehension of the details. Try to draw on and weave these details into your next reading with your child. Your child will respond well to hearing their own details in the stories, and these details will encourage their imagination even further. This will unfold even more when you read the next books in the series. Hence, by way of creative interaction with your child, you open up the door to their extraordinary inner wisdom and connect with their soul.

My daughters often enrich my meditations with little details and I use these to embellish my writing. Details, which add new dimensions to the meditations, and in many ways, they have made my kids co-authors of these booklets and other books, I have written. I love and respect this synergy. I encourage you to encourage an equal form of interaction at home with your child.

When working with and encouraging intuition and creativity with your child in this way, you really sense your child, as your child will sense you and feel that they are being heard and seen in a new and deeper way.

A feeling of coming home

As I see it, Chief Eaglefeather represents a part of our collective subconscious. He is part of our intuition and is stored inside us like an ancient collective wisdom. Since the beginning of time, water, earth and air - in their cleanest form - have taken part in life on earth. Later, man created fire, but even before this, we knew about the element fire from volcanoes, the sun and from inside Mother Earth. Chief Eaglefeather teaches us to find our way back to old know-how and how to create balance through our teachings of the elements.

In today's hectic society so many of us have forgotten - or rather repressed - this kind of knowledge deep within our subconscious minds.

Old wisdom

Through millennia the four elements have been used to cleanse the mind of human beings, consciously as well as unconsciously. The Greek philosophers spoke about the elements. As an example, Plato depicted the elements as geometrical figures known today as the platonic bodies. All the way up to the 18th century it was commonly known that all material was created using a combination of the four elements: Fire, Water, Earth and Air.

We encounter an interest for the elements in many old native cultures, religions and traditions across the globe, from Chinese medicine, via Taoism, yoga and astrology, to various indigenous people, such as Native Americans, Inuits and Maoris.

An old Maori saying goes:

"May Water cleanse you, May Air teach you, May Fire drive you, May Earth be a foundation for you".

In different cultures people connect, for instance, the cyclus of the day, zodiac signs, certain plants, gemstones, our bodily organs, and the seasons with the elements. If you have previously encountered the elements, you might also know about supplementary elements, such as wood and metal. In this book I have chosen to talk about the four elements that I know best and work with in my consultations.

It is my experience that many yearn to find their way back to the elements, and thus discover what an amazing and wonderful influence nature has on our mind and soul. Hence these meditations can provide us with a glorious feeling of coming home.

We had fun when we made
this book for you – we hope
you are having fun too.

About the author

The book series The Valley of Hearts is written by Gitte Winter Graugaard (b. 1977), who is also the author of the bestseller The Children's Meditations in my Heart and several other books.

Gitte is passionate about writing books to strengthen imagination in children, as well as nurture their intuition and create balance in life.

Gitte holds a Masters Degree in Business Administration and has worked in Communication, specialising in storytelling. She is also a trained Life Mastery Coach, Heartcore Mentor, Mindfulness Instructor and Conscious Transformer. Today she mainly shares her knowledge through intuitive storytelling and meditation.

However, the most important knowledge, namely to listen to yourself and live your dreams, originates in Gitte's own life, which is, and always has been, filled with love and choices of the heart.

www.gittewintergraugaard.dk

About the illustrator

Very often meditation opens up avenues for creativity. Elsie Ralston has illustrated these books. She was born and raised in Peru. Love for her husband brought her to Denmark. Below you can see a picture from the process of producing the illustrations for this book.

You can find Elsie on: www.elsieralston.com

Do you like drawing
with colours?

Now it's your turn - be creative!

Meditating with children often gives rise to good discussions. Write down some notes from your conversations in the back of the book. These notes may become very valuable to your child later in life.

On the following pages you will find the illustrations of the two meditations in this book in black and white as a special gift from Elsie. You can invite your child to draw his or her own version of the Valley of Hearts or colour the illustrations.

How did the valley look?

How did Chief Eaglefeather look?

Anything else you would like to draw today?

How did you sense the valley as you arrived in it? How did it look? You can colour and draw more details here.

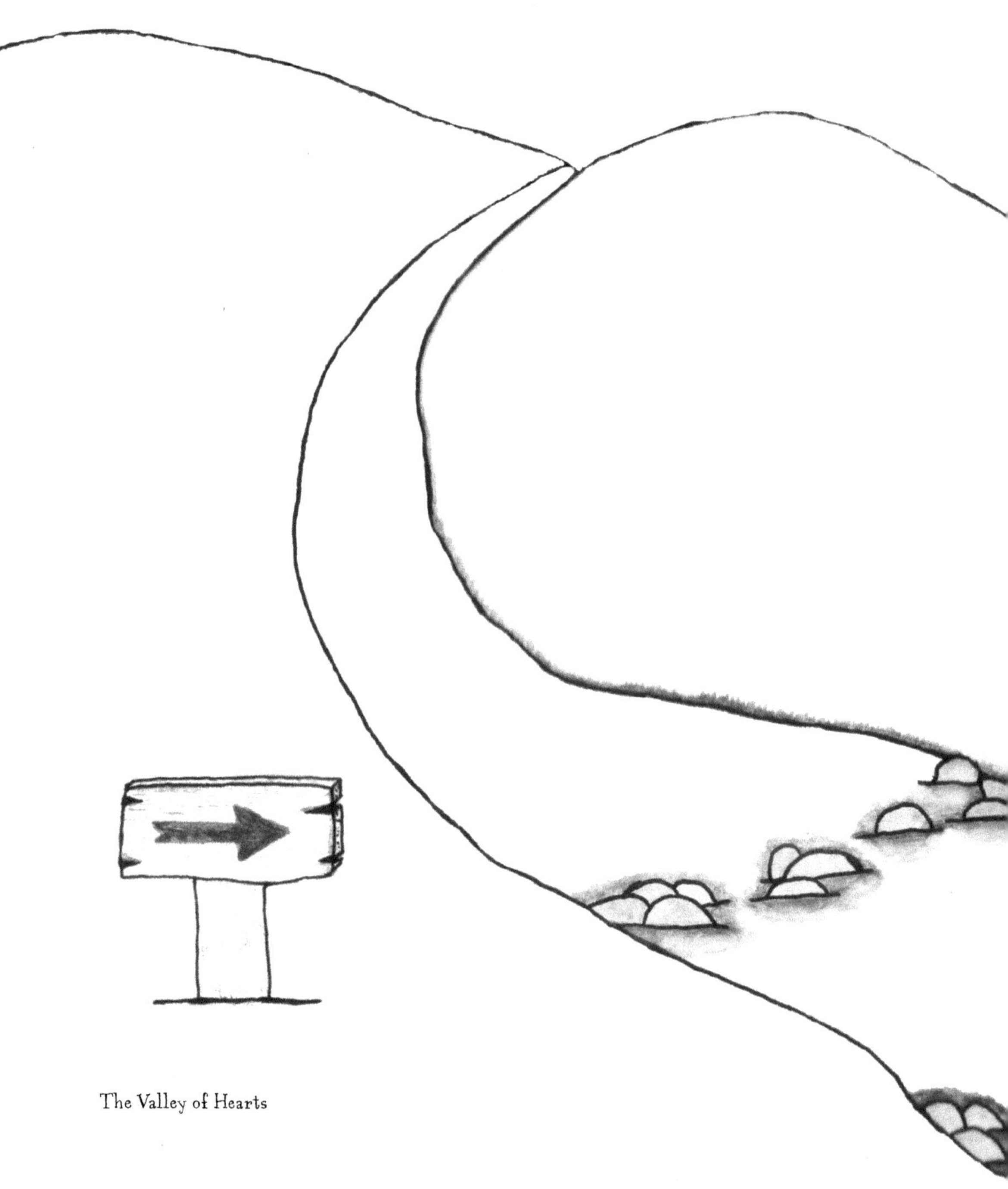

What do you think he is looking at? You can draw it if you like.

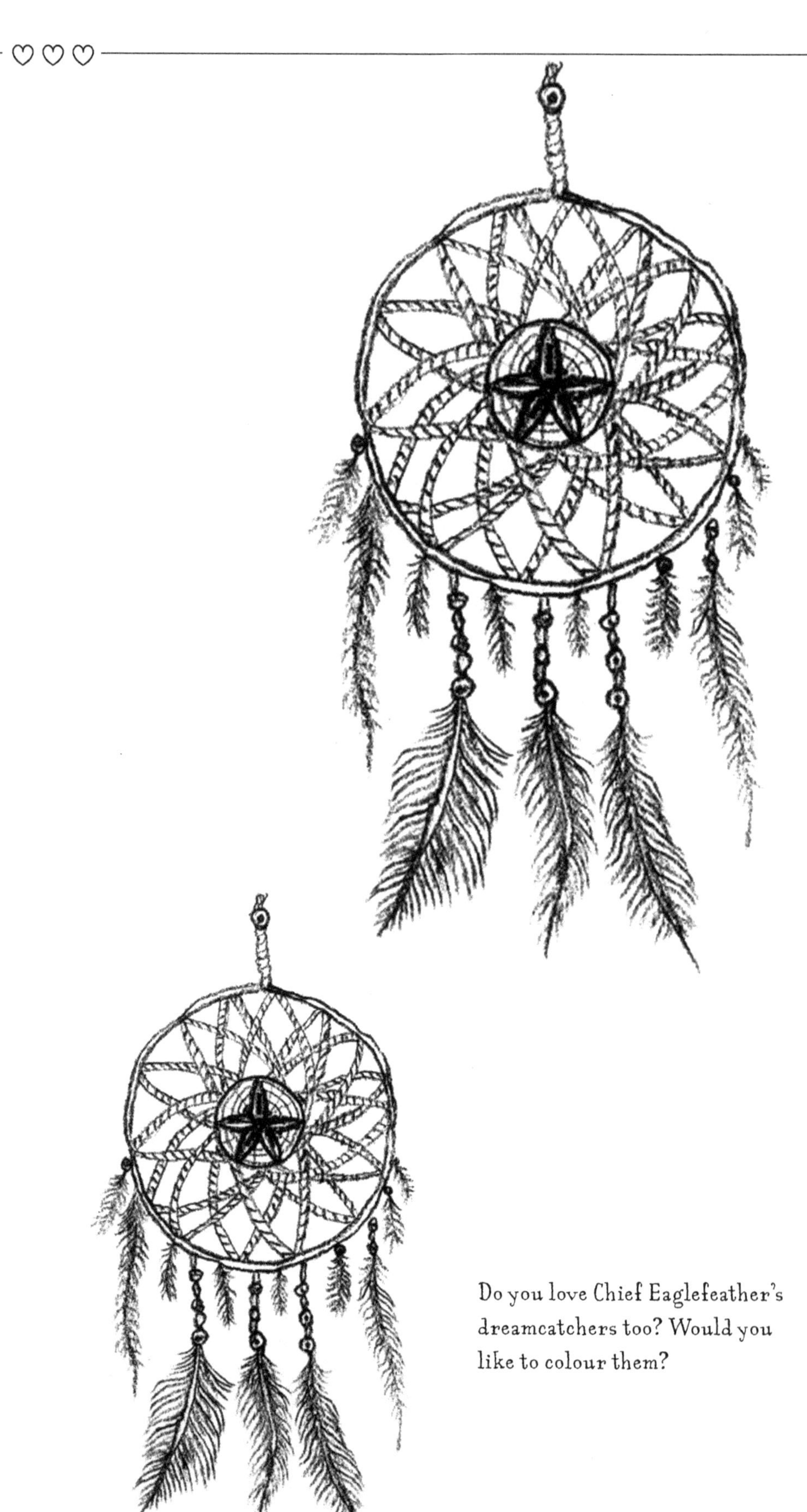

Do you love Chief Eaglefeather's dreamcatchers too? Would you like to colour them?

Design your own dreamcatcher

The Flamedancers' Fire

How did you see the valley, the river, the mountains and the tepee tents? Create you very own valley here.

The Clear Cascade

The Deep Meadow

The Mild Winds

The Valley of Hearts

Did you like meditating?

What did you like the most?

What did you like the most?

What do you dream
of when you
are sleeping?

Valuable notes for later in life...

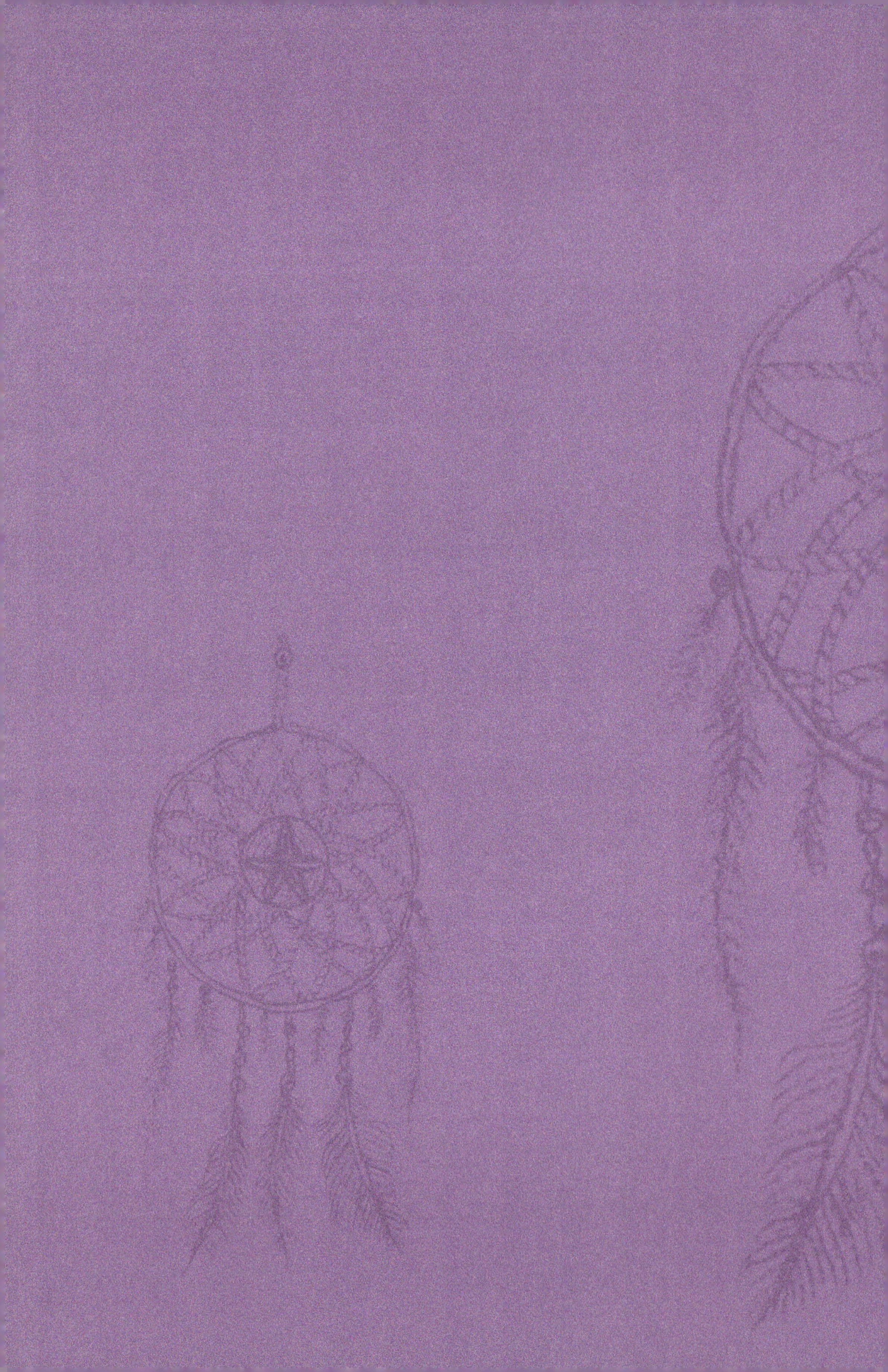

Did you like the
meditations and
would you like more?

Meet Chief Eaglefeather
Meditations for children
BEDTIME STORIES
Let sleep come easily with these meditations. Create a deep connection with your child and help them to recharge.
No 1
Gitte Winter Graugaard

The Flamedancers' Fire
Meditations for children
BEDTIME STORIES
Let sleep come easily with this FIRE meditation. Create a deep connection with your child and help them to recharge.
No 2

The Clear Cascade
Meditations for children
BEDTIME STORIES
Let sleep come easily with this WATER meditation. Create a deep connection with your child and help them to recharge.

The Deep Meadow
Meditations for children
BEDTIME STORIES
Let sleep come easily with this EARTH meditation. Create a deep connection with your child and help them to recharge.
No 4
Gitte Winter Graugaard

The Mild Winds
Meditations for children
BEDTIME STORIES
Let sleep come easily with this AIR meditation. Create a deep connection with your child and help them to recharge.
No 5
Gitte Winter Graugaard

All the books in the series The Valley of Hearts

In the first book, "Meet Chief Eaglefeather" I gave you two meditations.

As your child becomes more comfortable you can move further into the valley to encounter each of the elements. As you reach each new stage of the journey, new books and more meditations will be waiting for you.

"The Flamedancers' Fire" is book number two. You can benefit from using this meditation for children with lots of temper and conversely, for children with too little fire inside. Getting to know how to turn down or up your inner fire is crucial for how you cope in life.

"The Clear Cascade" in book number three is such a blessing to sensitive children and children prone to worry. It teaches us to cleanse our energy from other people before sleeping, which makes it a lot easier to feel our own energy and our own needs and boundaries.

Book number four is "The Deep Meadow", it is beneficial for all children in the Digital Age. Most children today need help to ground themselves.

We get to fly with "The Mild Winds" in book number five. The little daydreamers will love this meditation. However, it can also help children who need more perspective and creativity.

Each element has its own magical quality, which can be used to achieve peace of mind and to create better balance inside.

Please visit: www.thevalleyofhearts.com

The Children's Meditations

IN MY HEART

This bestselling book is teaching thousands of children to find their
Love Mountain and fill themselves with love. It works very well with
"Heartlight". You get four amazing meditations in one book.
They also help your child to sleep and teaches your child
about empathy, appreciation, connection and so much more.
Now selling in more than 20 countries in multiple languages.

www.inmyheart.eu

HEARTLIGHT

Teach your child to shine

This little book is an obvious sequel to "In My Heart", as the fifth
meditation. Here, your child learns to turn up their inner light
in the mountain of love and carry it around the whole body
to spread their inner light. This meditation is also part of
the book "The Monster Manual for children who worry a lot".
Find out how to make your child a light bearer.

www.heartlight.eu

A Global Mission

Gitte Winter Graugaard is on a mission to help ONE MILLION CHILDREN and their families thrive through bedtime meditation. She is an expert in peaceful bedtime routines. She is a bestselling and award-winning author, and a TEDx speaker.

Her books are helping thousands of children to sleep in more than 20 countries. Gitte always reminds us to parent ourselves first before we parent our children and become aware of what we radiate.

To find more inspiration to conscious parenting and
better sleep, you can follow Gitte's blog on:

www.gittewintergraugaard.dk

To book Gitte for speaking or workshops go to:

www.gittewintergraugaard.com

Gitte is on a mission
to teach 1 MILLION children
to meditate. You can help her
by sharing this book and your
experiences with others. Ask for
her books at your local library,
or at your favorite bookshop and
use as presents to those you love.

Support her mission.

See you soon ...

Thank you
for teaching
your child
to meditate.

CPSIA information can be obtained
at www.ICGtesting.com
Printed in the USA
BVHW022214290721
613187BV00014B/1094